Epiphany Kitchen

Copyright © 2017 by Victoria Verse

All rights reserved. No part of this book may be reproduced or transmitted in any form or by any means without written permission from the authors.

ISBN 978-1-7750822-2-4

Printed by IngramSpark (www.ingramspark.com)

ACKNOWLEDGEMENTS

Victoria Verse would like to thank everyone who contributed to and supported this publication. This is our first anthology of local poets and members of our group, and we are very excited to get our poems into the hands of our community.

We would like to thank Planet Earth Poetry for promoting the submission process.

Thank you to all of the Victoria Verse members (past and present) keeping poetry alive with your gentle words and insights.

A special thank you to Farah Percival for supplying the art work for the cover and individual sections in this publication.

Finally, thank you to all of the contributors to this anthology:

Adela Torchia	Nancy Yakimoski
Amy Nold	Peter Mancuso
Angela Lee McIntyre	Rosalind Taylor
A.S. Chan	Serafina Christina
Daymon Macmillan	Sydney Pimiskern
Delaney Levven	Tariq Al Lamki
Emily Krauss	Terra Hawk
Ibrahim Hazmi	Tina Johnston
Katherine Hewko	Torsten Schoeneberg
Michelle Riddle	

TABLE OF CONTENTS

I: NATURE SPEAKS IN POETRY 1

    On a Moonlit Night 2

    "... at all times within it ..." 3

    said the Ocean 4

    Sit by the Ocean 5

    Life of a Pebble 6

    Not 7

    Gone 7

    Forest Reflection 8

    Speak Not 9

    On the day the deer left the forest 10

    Naiad 11

    Wrap 12

    Nature's Joy 13

    September 14

    Pomegranate 14

    Windfall 15

    Maya Blue River 16

    There's a Garden in My Head 17

    Open 18

II: WE ARE ALL DYING, BUT ONLY SOME OF US MAKE MUSIC 19

    Sometimes I think my soul speaks Russian 20

    Lavender 22

    cinderella 23

    Fighting Denial 24

 Night 28

 Be Fearless 29

 Dear Love 30

III: OH HAIKUS! 32

 White Jasmine 33

 The Shore 33

 Mountains of the Moon 34

 Sleeping Chivalry 34

 Slumber Spectrum 35

 Untitled 35

 Alchemy 36

 Tag Annum 36

 Cherry trees, Victoria 37

 One Cloudy night 37

 Waiting 38

 Untitled 38

IV: IN THE BOOK OF NIGHT 39

 This Nightly Shriving 40

 A Question of Day and Night 41

 My Friend, the Night 42

 Moon Beams 43

 These Longest Nights 44

 Crème brûlée 45

 Candlelight 46

V: DON'T MIND ME 47

 Wiggle, Fidget and Squirm 48

Addiction 50

Lookin' for Myself 51

Young 52

Origin 53

Ad Model 54

Sungazing 55

This Longing 56

VI: WHERE ARE WE NOW? 59

Ode to the Keyboard 60

Penn's Woods 62

A Spoonful of the Matrix 63

Donning the Armour (after the Trump election) 64

Rumi on Yates Street 66

At Mt. Baldy 68

Yogini 69

Stormborn 70

VII: SWEET LIGHT AND LOVE 74

Sweet Morning Tea 75

She Spreads Her Wings 76

Light Rider 77

Untitled 77

his house for her (Alexander's Castle, Fort Worden, WA) 78

Love Sparks 79

Speechless 80

October Reverie 81

New Act 81

Fools and Angels 81
Epiphany Kitchen 82
Tenth Planet Love 83
توأمُ الرُّوحِ (Soul-Mate) 83
أسطورةُ الرُّوح (Saga of the Soul) 86
حصارٌ .. (Siege ..) 88
خيبةُ الأسئلةِ (Disappointments of "Whys") 92
قولي كما شئتِ (As you wish) 94
قبري على وقفةٌ (Standing At My Grave) 97
بُرُودٌ .. (Iceberg) 101
قولي كما شئت (Mutiny) 103
ما الفرقُ بينكما ؟! .. (The difference between you) 105
خلودٌ .. (Eternity) 108

VII: AT LAST, WORDS 111

Spade 112
Petals 113
Silence 114
Two with the Word "Carve" 115
Reverse Blade 116
Ode to Frost 117
forefinger and thumb 118
Swoon 119
Solitary Traveller 122
blessing name 123

INDEX OF AUTHORS 124

I: NATURE SPEAKS IN POETRY

On a Moonlit Night
By Terra Hawk

And there sat the cat
Awash in the moonlight

Green eyes focused on a rat

Tiny nails skittered *tat-tat*
Slinking through the night

And there sat the cat

Scenting French fries from a vat
The rodent crunched, with appetite

Green eyes focused on a rat

The alley-trash acrobat
 Dining in delight

And there sat the cat

Stuffed it scampered *pitter-pat*
The cat tensed, taking flight

Green eyes focused on a rat

With a crack and a splat
Dead without a fight

And there sat the cat
Green eyes focused on a rat

"... at all times within it..."
a line from *Three Times My Life Has Opened* by Jane Hirshfield
By Angela Lee McIntyre

From this forest trail I see how
we remember, recognize ourselves
when we let go. It's easy to forget that,
easy to forget how easy it is to be with the truth
that is already here. It doesn't matter where you go
or who you are, you'll always have the wind to move a branch
call forth undulating ripples of light at your feet
the maps and stories on the forest's floor
that you absorb and know.

At all times within it, I believed you, like I would a deer or a knife.
Maybe you believed it, too.

At all times within it, the forest rests on the legs of beetles, roots,
its own debris. At all times within it, the forest captures and releases,
shelters. At all times within it, the forest rises up, expands and falls,
breathing us in at all times, within it.

said the Ocean
By Nancy Yakimoski

I love you like Icarus
    like the choking stink of scorched feathers
    the intoxicating perfume of melting beeswax

I love you like the dizzy adrenalin buzz of flight
    soaring without regard for safety or consequence
    contraption collapsing: tangle of feathers, buckles, and wood

        taking the plummet and
        falling head first in
        ahhhhhhhhhh
        love.

I love you like the inevitable crash
    the head snap-cracking backwards on impact
    the blinding white then dark breathless silence
    the motionless surrender

        drifting

      sinking

      into the endless murky arms

      of my love.

Sit by the Ocean
By Emily Krauss

Sit by the ocean,
And listen to the waves, crashing aggressively,
Against the jagged and grey rocks.
Watch the fierce waves,
Rumble in the water after a ferryboat passes by.
See the birch trees swaying back and forth
in the wind,
and watch the seagulls dive for ocean treasures.

Sit by the ocean,
And listen to the waves, crashing aggressively,
Against the jagged and grey rocks.
Feel the warmth of the sand
oozing between your toes.
Smell the fresh salt in the air
that is all around you.
Let nature engulf your entire body
into the spirit of the great outdoors.

Sit by the vast and lonely ocean,
Listen with all your might to the waves,
Crashing aggressively, against,
the jagged and grey rocks.
Watch the mango orange sunset appear
like magic in the evening sky
and enjoy living in this moment.

Life of a Pebble
By Farah Percival

Holding tight to the eroding shore -
Which path to follow isn't a choice anymore.
      Damp pebble - *stuck in a ripple*
      Made smooth by a gentle drizzle

It can be rough, being tossed and rolled
Down a wild course that can't be controlled.
      Grainy pebble - *meek and little*
      Made smooth by a gentle drizzle

Distant fears swirl 'round and back,
As reliably as the night is black.
      Stony pebble - *strong though brittle*
      Made smooth by a gentle drizzle

Washed into a lasting groove -
In deep waters that do not move.
      River pebble - *sleek and simple*
      Made smooth by a gentle drizzle

Not
By Rosalind Taylor

i had a dream it was spring
the birds had returned
i heard the blossomed sky once again
and i will not write about war

i had a dream it was spring
couples held ungloved hands
i felt the live lawn in bare feet
and i will not write about war

i had a dream it was spring
the air was a crisp green apple
i drank peppermint tea on the porch
and i will not write about war

Gone
By Sydney Pimiskern

I gladly go galloping through the grass
My graceful locks, glowing, glimmering, shine
Gusts of wind greatly gain mass
Grazing my main I whine
Higher I go
Grateful, I gallop
Gaining speed to go to God

Forest Reflection
By Emily Krauss

Deep in the forest,
Full of evergreen, birch and oak trees
Is where you can find me
Sitting by the warm clear water
Dipping my feet
And feeling the wetness
Surround my toes

I'm all alone
Not a soul nearby
Not a creak
Nor a rustle in the bushes
No footsteps can be heard
Just me, my breathing and my thoughts

It's what I relish once in awhile
As I just let myself, reflect and meditate
About life in general and the world

Speak Not
By Terra Hawk

Speak not of darkling forests
Nor the pounding of the sea
Or rain-swept mountain passes
Speak of naught to me

Speak not of clouds and sunbursts
Or singing birds at dawn
Speak not of love nor beauty
For my heart's already gone

On the day the deer left the forest
By Michelle Riddle

On the day the deer left the forest, not a tear was shed.

No witness watched to report that the day was bright, the air was crisp, and bees built hives between tree roots. Nobody could confirm that the squirrels nattered at one another and predators lurked in shadow.

On the day the deer left the forest, no one laughed aloud.

If someone had seen, but no one did, how they stood erect and put top hats on their heads and bowties on their tails, they might have suspected something was wrong, they might have found it funny, they might have wondered if the bees and the squirrels and the foxes understood.

On the day the deer left the forest, none thought to ask.

Would the wolves become vegetarians? Would thick bark trunks be the new look for trees? Would the ants build a canopy-high temple for their queen? Would cougars take up mah jong and robins make art of discord?

On the day the deer left the forest, nothing heard them go.

They laced ballet slippers around their dainty legs and leapt and twirled out through the bramble and leaves, shaking ripe summer fruit from the trees that bore such bounty, though not an apple, cherry, nor a plum kept them from passing beyond the green border.

On the day the deer left the forest, nobody said a prayer.

And the scrub took over. Hikers stopped wandering off the public paths, hunters made sport of themselves, and campers became the subtle subject of nature photography.

On the day the deer left the forest, not a thing was missed.

Because everyone knows that the forest holds gentle, amber-eyed grace that, when it's sought, can only be found at the periphery of vision.

Naiad

By Michelle Riddle

In a pond I saw the sky
With dreamy clouds floating by.
In the sky I saw the rain
Filling up the pond again.

Wrap

By Rosalind Taylor

Wrap the long sweet pea
vine around your waist
so you may always be held
warm hand of the sun
on your back, green vine
rising to braid your hair
and crest as a crown,
blossom resting on your forehead
your every turn perfumed

Wrap the still forest
floor around your feet
so you may always be held
cool carpet of moss between
your toes, morning dew drops rest
at your forehead diamonds at dawn
radiance ringing your gaze
all you see is light
and all you see is light

Nature's Joy
By Sydney Pimiskern

Blades of grass are ballerinas
Dancing perfectly in place
To the beat of the wind.

Their sister trees, rooted and strong,
Moved by nothing by the wind, and forever growing tall.
This breeze sings its way around the world,
Stopping in the valleys to visit cousin waters.
Rivers feed stallions
That thunder and froth and gather speed
Racing to the lake where they are at peace with their mother.
Until she sends them down stream,
For more growing up to do.

September
By Farah Percival

I

Am surrounded

By August leaves

Even in the changing

Season. But for her, the

Months of green have already

Transitioned to autumn reds -

During the first

Week of

September.

Pomegranate
By Katherine Hewko

Late summer burden
Boozy stench split open
Unzipped
Sticky, bloody pearls spill forth across the orchard
Sour juice staining the soil
Grenadine carnage

Windfall
By Michelle Riddle

> *Hefted sails training toward shore*
> *Fill up hearts with amorous score,*
> *Whether of home or distant shore.*
> *Windfall waits at every door,*
> *Of this, oh Muse, do I implore.*

When the wind falls
the pasture stills
into its slumbering fallow
to keep the pace,
the peace of the times.
In country counterbalance,
cattle sandwiches and chicken coop soup
make three-dimensional eclogue economical.
The laboured land belongs to the pickers,
whose momentary summer spectre
flits away, like swallowtail butterflies,
before the berries rot at the roadside
produce stands attracting all those weekend vacationers:
the proverbial fly on the proverbial Walden Pond.

But the winds will pick
up over placid, plastic-packed waters
where sunbathers practice their sun block slathered social obedience.
The winds will rise
to stir the sedentary heart, not
with the forgotten fury of the undying gods,
but with the lyre of mourning, raw as the red dawn.
Those immortal breasts will not heave
for Her, our bountiful home,
but for us, for mortal misery
miserly chosen without regard for choice:
the free wild wind of will
to bend, and not to break,
the windfall.

Maya Blue River
By Farah Percival

Curvaceous Maya Blue River

    Smooth as luxury silk sliver

   Simple, sophisticated glow

Floodplains of wisdom you bestow

    Curvaceous Maya Blue River

    Ample vitality giver

      Gleaming, moving beings below

       Floodplains of wisdom you bestow

      Curvaceous Maya Blue River

     Excited, refreshing shiver

   Cool natural beauty on show

Floodplains of wisdom you bestow

Curvaceous Maya Blue River

  Always a gentle, light quiver

    Streams of ageless knowledge you know

      Floodplains of wisdom you bestow

There's a Garden in My Head
By Peter Mancuso

There's a garden in my head,
Where I keep all things precious to me.
There's a garden in my head,
Growing as far as my mind can see.

In the garden is truth and love,
In forms fantastic, beautiful, and free,
In the garden is truth and love,
In shapes that I forever want to see.

There at the garden's heart, you will find
Gilded apples, glinting with reflected lights.
There at the garden's heart, you will find
Each apple reflecting the garden's delights.

Open
By Rosalind Taylor

The gate has opened
To the forest path
What mysteries here
What delights?

The flowers have opened
To the ripening sun
What colours here
What sights?

The sea has opened
To the fullest moon
What shadows here
What whites?

All eyes have opened, all eyes have seen
And all the eyes are bright.

II: WE ARE ALL DYING, BUT ONLY SOME OF US MAKE MUSIC

Sometimes I think my soul speaks Russian
By Torsten Schoeneberg

    Sometimes I think my soul speaks Russian
I can't quite understand what she says.
"Psyche", I beg her
(I call her "Psyche", like the Ancients and Edgar Allan did),
"Psyche, speak to me clearly,
in German, French or English, in Latin or Greek if you will,
or let me make dinner!" –
but she won't, she'll never, she will
mumble blunt syllables while I cut leek.

    Yet I know she has in the past
quietly killed off my fears
or replaced them with better ones;
so I consent and go on, hoping she'll speak
some Western language again when I need her; until then
only when we watch a film by Tarkovsky
or when I read to her from Chekhov, or Handke,
she sometimes nods as if hinting
"See? That's what I mean", and allows me to sleep.

    Last month we watched a dying musician in concert:
She heard what was sung and said
but does not like shows, so when they
showed the Prime Minister applauding, she just grinned
waiting with ulterior reservations.
(Being misbehaved and illegal,
she'd get deported, from everywhere and Russia,
if she were by herself.)
Then she kept nagging when people uttered "how special, he's dying"
till I asked her straight to the face: What is it?
She just shook her head quietly
but later, in bed, she whispered –
        Don't you feel it's strange
        We are all dying
        But only some of us make music.

Lavender
By Torsten Schoeneberg

    What is the difference between happiness and plucking lavender?

Let me tell you.

    If you asked me, "When was the last time you plucked lavender?"

I could say: Last Sunday

For an hour or so in the afternoon,

On a black plastic garbage bag in our carport

Pulling off leaves until my fingers got itchy

Thinking of maps, and schooldays, and spiders

And greeting, like they did, all neighbours

Except for the grumpy one.

    But if you asked me,

"When was the last time you felt happiness?"

I could get grumpy

And feel the need to go home

To read Wittgenstein on our couch, with lavender on the table

And never be sure what to say.

cinderella
By Nancy Yakimoski

my embers my ashes my cinder
Ella just wanted a seaside holiday alone
barefoot, bikinied
reading books, writing poems
drinks holding tiny paper umbrellas
and no ever-afters

instead, the desert
bleached skull moonlight guarding
hunger-driven work
spider is spinning, she's writing
"cannibalism"

her finger traces the prince's scar
from his back to ribcage to bellybutton
like the winding road leading into Albuquerque
(like the cold desert outside to the kiva fire inside)
like the winding road leading out of Albuquerque

he says, *now that I've found you, fall in love with me*
she thinks, that's not how it's supposed to happen

at the airport,
she promises they will see each other again
fingers are crossed

lies, truths and other sweet nothings, glass
slipper, jet fuel propulsion, pumpkin
dreams; there are no brakes

Fighting Denial
By Delaney Levven

He uses a shovel to dig a large hole,
Deeper and deeper, down he goes,
He uses that shovel to throw in half truths,
Stashing and stuffing them into that groove.

Using that shovel, he covers them up,
Piling and packing dirt into that rut.
With that same shovel he carries his lies,
Stacking, amassing them, top out of sight.

He then uses a tool to sculpt out a dream,
takes you to that pile of lies to see
An easy-on-the-eyes type of fantasy;
Taking you a fool, trying to make you believe.

He is taken aback when you simply shatter
That dream with an axe, shards of lies scatter
And pierce a veil that kept everyone blind,
You made their eyes see, including mine

Those truths once carefully stashed away,
Truths uncovered when innocence is claimed,
Hard truths to which we look away,
Truths you uncover and refuse to let fade,

Why do you do this?
> I've told you before.

Tell me again, tell me once more.

Tell me again why you would dare
To strip my world of colour bare.
Tell me again why, in doing what you did,
You'd knock those tinted glasses off my head.

Why you'd remind me that my 'friends'
Are merely convenient acquaintances.
And why you won't let me pretend and
Strip the candied coat off my medicine,

Especially when it's too much to handle,
When you know that's why we accept these scandals,
When you know those lies are used as props,
That these truths have no resolve?

You let me vent, you let me cry.
You let me finish, before you reply:

> Because every time you expect the beautiful,
> He slaps you hard, he slaps you cold.
> Because every time you wear those frames,
> He sneaks up from behind and inflicts pain.

Every time you lend the unworthy your trust,
You're left behind, you're left in the dust.
And every time you take his prescription
He presents a utopia – a false depiction.

He lets you freefall into a pit of shards
Of illusory lies that leave behind scars,
And it hurts so much, you need an escape
So you take his solution, knowing it's fake.

Taking his shovel and using your beliefs,
Like a tool to make others see what you see,
He lures you all to take that climb
Atop all his lies, so lovely, divine.

He builds you, he molds you,
He uses you, controls you.
And he'll continue to, so long as you're able,
But what he builds is always unstable.

Piling lies higher than ever before
To cover old wounds that'd left you sore,
He sculpts those lies into plausible conjecture,
But due to their overpromising nature,

Those lies eventually contradict,
Creating false footholds, making you slip
From those tales piled ever so tall.
You fall harder every subsequent fall,

Cutting deeper and closer to your core.
Rather than ease your pain, you end up with more.
But he takes you a fool, your trust again he earns
Making you forget. When will you learn

His cunning ways, his sneaky devices?
His pathological nature, manipulating your vices?
His ability to soothe you, despite all you've lost?
Despite all of your incurring costs

His beautiful lies you continue to buy,
But you know better - want to know how I know why?
Because within you, at a level gut-deep
Remains what rings true, represented through me.

I'm that voice, I'm your conscience
I sort through his ridiculous nonsense
Hacking away at his substance-less banter
To get at the truth, the heart of the matter.

And despite all his attempts and protests
They're of no use, for I will not rest.
Instead, I take his shovel and tools
And propose that we build something *anew*
On truths.

Night
By Daymon Macmillan

a cold green shiver with bat wings for eyes
our baby boy
product of belly and seed
comes tottering between
argument and sleep

comes bumping into the bedroom
dares me to look at him
nurse him
trade him bruises for a handful of band-aids

it used to worry me you'd wake up
my cryptic breath
stinging the back of your neck
while I held him

broken
our bag of splinters and ice
still begs a lullaby

Be Fearless
By Serafina Christina

Be fearless when

Choosing love

Even if it hurts.

Be fearless when

Choosing kindness

Even if it's hard.

Be fearless when

Choosing to shine

Even if it's scary.

Be fearless when

Choosing joy

Even when it's different.

Be fearless when

Choosing vulnerability

Even when no one else does.

Dear Love
By Sydney Pimiskern

I never understood love -
A desire to be held,
Like an apple longing to be picked,
Before it is rotten and falls.
Someone to raise me up,
Like a penguin
Running fast with flippers while flapping flightless wings.
If love makes you so strong,
Then why does it make us so vulnerable,
Like a butterfly's wings, fresh from the cocoon?

Love is unique.

It must be cared for like anything in this world.
It is a beautiful crisp apple,
But we must be ready to pick it.
It is like the flippers of a penguin,
Used to keep its baby warm and protected.
It is like a butterfly's wings,
Fragile,
But can climb great heights.
Love is embracing what is in front of you.
Love is easy to understand.

Parallel lines, two profiles
simple as day rising

separate, distinct
yet in close tandem

the empty space between them
tango

of strait and fjord
wave surge.

I hold the drawing in my hand,
a locket, simple as day rising.

Once opened I know, I know
surf will arc forth, sun-tangled

and night's longing.
Be, oh be . . . enough.

III: OH HAIKUS!

White Jasmine
By Rosalind Taylor

returning home late

fragrant jasmine blossom falls

long white sun grown cold

The Shore
By Peter Mancuso

We wait on the shore,

The thin bubble of our lives,

Small against the sea.

Mountains of the Moon
By Farah Percival

The Mountains of the

Moon, covered their peaks with a

Thousand white crystals

Sleeping Chivalry
By Peter Mancuso

Rising from the mists,

A castle sleeps, dreaming of

Knights and princesses.

Slumber Spectrum
By Peter Mancuso

Colours blaze and fade;

A forest dreams of springtime

Reflecting on green.

Untitled
By Rosalind Taylor

pumpkins in the field

October's red still warm sough

cloudless black bird flies

Alchemy
By Michelle Riddle

Winter jasmine gold

makes love without a volta -

a silent sonnet.

Tag Annum
By Peter Mancuso

Old Year slouches past,

Patting New Year on the head.

"You'll do just fine, kid."

Cherry trees, Victoria
By Nancy Yakimoski

Each Spring I'm a bride

walking down this city's aisles

confetti petals

One Cloudy night
By Peter Mancuso

On a cloudy night

A whale, a sub, and a ship

Passed by in the sky

Waiting
By Peter Mancuso

Wooden tree-dancer,

Her graceful limbs lifted high,

Waiting for a breeze.

Untitled
By Peter Mancuso

The forest path wends,

Taking a cool green journey

To places unseen.

IV: IN THE BOOK OF NIGHT

This Nightly Shriving
By Rosalind Taylor

The garden's coloured blooms

peeled back, black

the Forest takes off all her myriad greens,

flayed to shapes

The heavy chatter of day birds now quiet,

still

Owl calls, softer

a lover's breath

ear to chest

familiar and measureless mystery

The conifers are lace

against a Moon-bright sky

laid bare, exquisite

this nightly shriving

A Question of Day and Night
By Angela Lee McIntyre

In lockdown — I need time
to contemplate the meaning of a racing heart.

I see my heart
only beats with love
there is no other
truth.

Unmoving, unmoved,
unbidden, unused
time wants
to be used,
with or without you.

Do you love the day or the night?
I love the night for coming to hold me, when it comes
the day for always forgetting.

What is that sound?
The orange objects in this room — a dog's toy and one part of the
pattern on the carpet and my cell phone case — are singing.

What do you see?
Ancient stones fold and open along the shore,
bright green seaweed softens their broken hearts.

My Friend, the Night
By Amy Nold

I love my friend, the night.

She comes on ever longer visits this time of year, and wraps me in Her velvety cloak of darkness, and hides me in Her wing.

Tucked in, I am like a child again, all innocence and wonder and marvel and trepidation for the Great Unknown.

That expanse laid before me, hiding all, hiding nothing.

She lays to rest the busyness of Her sister, Summer, and while I warm my bones around the hearth, She tells me stories of ancestral memories of survival.

She lets me know that I Am part of her and that Nothing is more constant than Her return.

Then She invites me to curl up in a warm comforter and lay down my head on soft pillows, while She lulls me to sweet sleep.

I listen to the nourishing rains pour liquid life from the sky onto our Earth as I prepare for my nightly journey inside Her darkly illuminated heart.

Moon Beams
By Michelle Riddle

Hanging from the winter branches
Grey with dusking light
A ripened plum swells
With golden pleasures of summer.
Bow limbs creak and moan
A woodwind lullaby to leaves
Trembling farewell and drifting into silence.
She falls up --
A delicious unplucked fruit
Bearing her seed into darkened heavens.
Rising still she falls
Savoured only by the glassy pond,
That rests her upon the earth
And knows day best in the deep of night.

These Longest Nights
By Rosalind Taylor

When the wind throws barbed ice
along the ridge, and in the twisting
indigo forest, even Hope could lose
its way, tumble somewhere
down slick banks
toward the long silent creek.

Still here, under once tended mulch
and faint fragrant pine needles
deep bulbs spin in slow dreams
condensed colours in the close,
close black.

An irrepressible song in the breaking
Soft-lidded centre of your heart,
a timpani skin, rising
winter moth wings,
sound pushing through dark blood,
light pulsing in the breaking, rings out
through delicate fluting tears,
sings out these longest nights
and it's this, your song
that beats the stars to shine.

Tear [tair]: to rip, divide or disrupt by the pull of opposing forces.

Crème brûlée
By Michelle Riddle

Light limned evening streets
swell with laughing high heeled chatter
in the last act of the long city day play.
Piqued savory red curtain scents
send glowing candlelit invitations
to enraptured friends and eighth time lovers.
Ex-business partners strike up new
romances to the beer buzzed call of TV sport spectators.
A lonely traveler cozies in a corner to sip from
smutty Kindle contents while the clink, tink, clatter
come hum tempts patrons passing windows swung siren wide.
Student cafe conversations punctuate perfunctory thought or
provoke retreat into the sonic silence of a private headset.
Sofas softly caress kids and creators slipping into
lulled wool woven legends in second story dens.

Standing black against star studded space,
the crow perched on rooftop ledge waits
to feast on the this sweet palette.

Candlelight
By Michelle Riddle

In candlelight a new world is born.

A world fringed in shadow.

A world of dark fairy wings that smooth the edges of firey light and cast

A veil over searching eyes: a veil of secrets, a veil of mystery, a veil of sight in a lightless land.

In candlelight little demons dance.

They flick their fire tongues, singing sanguine charms of forever perfect moments, of burning

Lovers, of lovers burning like little demons.

In candlelight stars watch people like people watch stars and they make

Wishes on shooting people and map their place in the universe

Relative to continental constellations.

In candlelight a tiny day is resurrected in the cold of night.

Cast aside by this baby phoenix, the night presses in to be burned away,

Thrown back to the shadow, though she never ceases her unspoken lullaby.

And when the phoenix returns to ash,

She wraps the world in her star down comforter of darkness.

V: DON'T MIND ME

Wiggle, Fidget and Squirm
Tina Johnston

I shook my head

Left and right.

I wrinkled my forehead

Up and down.

I winked my eyes

Open and closed.

I wiggled my nose

Side to side.

I puckered my lips

In and out.

I turned my neck

Left and right.

I shrugged my shoulders

Up and down.

I lifted my arms

In and out.

I waved my hands

Side to side.

I bent my waist

Up and down.

I wiggled my bum

Left and right.

I tucked my knees

In and out.

I rotated my ankles

Round and round.

I stomped my foot

Up and down.

Then I sat down on the floor

And didn't shake, wink, bend, stomp,

Wiggle, fidget or squirm.

Addiction

By Farah Percival

The

Addictions of

A secret temptress

With a lustful touch

A secret alcoholic with empty

Bottles of whiskey and rum

She loved many men

And he loved

Sweet poison

- Addiction

Lookin' for Myself
By Amy Nold

Lookin' for myself for such a long long time
I want to find myself
I don't know what I'll find
I hope I find somebody new
I'm tired of bein' blue.

I seem so hard to find
I don't know where to look,
I could be in my mind
I could be in a book

My thoughts are scattered everywhere,
It's almost more than I can bear
Lookin,' lookin' all around.

If I'm looking for myself
Then why can't I be found?
Could it be I don't know where to look?
Maybe, just maybe I'm not in a book

What's this I hear you say? I shouldn't follow your way?
You say my truth is to be found
By finding my own feet on the ground.

So now I'm on my way
I think I've found myself
Here's what I have to say
C'mon, get off the shelf!

Dust off those gifts of yours
Unlock and open up the doors.
'Cause you are where you are
So hang tight, just stay put,
Don't need to go too far
There's no place else to look.
Everything's inside of you
I wouldn't lie, I'm telling you true!
Yeah, yeah, yeah, yeah, everything's inside of you.

Young
By Sydney Pimiskern

You were too young to die.
You sung from every hill top.
You clung to every hug.
I would have rung the angel away.
Told heaven they could wait another day.
Wrung from the loss of you,
My lung ceases to breathe.
My heart stung and still stings.
Why are the young to die?

Origin

By Amy Nold

The explosion, the Big Bang

that takes place at the Beginning of Creation

where sperm meets egg and the encoding of each join together

to inform the unfolding of Spirit into Matter, and birth the encoded information into life forms - You, I, Everything - the Original Yoga

Gestalted in the universal womb of darkness

Who is this Mother?

Who is this Father?

that through their union give birth to the

Whole Creation?

Ad Model
By Delaney Levven

Piercing eyes of uncommon tone

Stare directly into my own,

Underneath layers of hair so fine

In colour and texture, exquisite, divine,

Complimenting that fair skin tan

Those perfectly blushed cheeks. Out stand

Your luscious lips, rose and upturned

Revealing that smile, oh how I yearn

To approach you, get to know you, eventually well

Outside of what it is you're trying to sell

Perhaps to begin, a greeting, then an exchange

Between you and I, of our names

A means to identify each other with

But before I do, I take a minute

And suddenly ask out of cue,

Are your colours true?

Sungazing

By Farah Percival

Share

Something, anything

Beautiful sungazing goddess

Even if all your

Unspoken words are uncontrollable tears

This Longing
By Amy Nold

Have you ever let go of something

Just because you cared so much

That it hurt to think it just won't work,

It's asking too much?

Too much of your heart, your soul,

Your blood,

Your breath,

Your grit,

Your sweat,

That you feel you can't dig deep enough

To find what's asked of you?

> *And this longing, that you yearn for,*
>
> *Will it ever come to be?*
>
> *How much do you care,*
>
> *And what will you share*
>
> *For your reality?*

Have you ever felt your heart break

Just because you cannot see

What you need from day to day

To keep your spirit inspired?

And this thing called Life, it changes,

It gives us what we bring to it.

So nurture seeds in fertile earth,

Labour long to give birth.

> *And this longing, that you yearn for,*
>
> *Will it ever come to be?*
>
> *How much do you care,*
>
> *And what will you share*
>
> *For your reality?*
>
> *It's so far in there just to find*
>
> *What is living there inside*
>
> *The flesh, the bones, ancestor's blood:*
>
> *The lotus rises from the mud.*

Let me take your hand, your heart,

I'll help you while you're blown apart,

And in the land of between dreams,

Where nothing's as it seems,

Some of my dreams have come true

While others never had a chance.

How much is based on what we do?

How much is happenstance?

>*And this longing, that you yearn for,*
>
>*Will it ever come to be?*
>
>*How much do you care,*
>
>*And what will you share*
>
>*For your reality?*
>
>*It's so far in there just to find*
>
>*What is living there inside*
>
>*The flesh, the bones, ancestor's blood:*
>
>*The lotus rises from the mud.*

>>*Dig in deep, don't go to sleep, try to find the jewel inside.*
>>
>>*Dig in deep, don't go to sleep, try to find the jewel inside.*
>>
>>*Dig in deep, don't go to sleep, try to find the jewel inside.*

VI: WHERE ARE WE NOW?

Ode to the Keyboard
By Angela Lee McIntyre

the here, now, of the asdfghjkl;

or the here, now of the qwertyuio[uio[

left out the p

poor p

return

return

return' (plus a small bird)

my bones moving inside my typing fingers, someone says they are

I like the slippery feel under my fingerprints

if this weren't typing, what would it be

digging in the dirt?

my dog buries things and then forgets where they are

have I forgotten and dig to remember?

the palm curves over and maybe I'm playing the piano, now I hear the music of n o w I h e a r t h e m u s i c

a show tune!

air on the back of my hands and they tingle as they write these words

music slides through and out,

some old need to make music,

this song like a tap tap tapping of the crows

on the roof

how does a wrist participate? the butt of my hands hold the wrists up off the

ledge of the laptop, that part of the computer that has no name, brother

a lower back that curves towards and away,

depending on your point of view, and legs

that delight in being prepared for anything

shoulders that know you

and love you, a neck

and face that carries glasses, eyeballs, a tongue

all resting for now, here

Penn's Woods
By Katherine Hewko

Sizzling stink of manure rushes the rental car's air conditioner
Lowering the windows offers no escape.
It's 102F and muggy, humid, sultry
Inching down the highway behind a convoy of Plain buggies
Like the ants who go marching.

Father shouts and Mother shushes
Brother and sister impinge on the smallest sliver
Claimed by the smallest kid in the middle of the backseat
Cramped and volatile like matches in a box.

Winding return to those who gave three skinny towheaded children
And their wan WASP mother
Too ethnic a name.

How to account for a man who smokes in defiance of the First Lady?
Or a woman who relies utterly upon father, brother, husband, son
Because girls Can't?

The pale sullen girl wades in the creek
Keeping a wary eye on father and brother,
Quick and violent tempers are their inheritance from this place.
Dark mud sucks the rubber flipflops off her arctic white feet
And the gravel scorches her toes on the dash home
To the museum piece house.

America sleeps here.
America paused here in 1949.
We celebrate a kind of freedom with a parade
And a racist slur in the next breath.
Venerating the past in which we are complicit.
We close the shutters of our minds
Against the burning funereal heat.

A Spoonful of the Matrix
By Tariq Al Lamki

I am a spoonful of the matrix;
Will you bend?
I am the beauty of the beast.
I fly over the no fly zone of the cuckoo's nest.
The wind goes with me.
The wolves dance with me.
I am the laughter of the lambs.
I will take the Decimus to the Maximus!
I am the Edge of Darkness.
Feel the embrace of my Lethal Weapon 4.
I have come to put an X on your men.
When I come; the tiger crouches,
And the dragon hides.
Come dragon, I will train you in 3D.
Tiger stay,
In my eye.
I am unbreakable.
I am the will inside Bruce.
I am die hard.
I am Sam.
I am Legend.
I am all of the terminators.
I have lost my Bourne identity.
I walk the Green Mile alone.
I am Cast Away;
I run like Forest in the jungle.
I am hunting good will.
I am searching for the truth.
With it; I will unite the Gangs of New York.

I come from the tribes beyond the wall.
I am the First Samurai.
I will take the Aurelius to the Maximus!
Rome was just a whisper;
Now hear me roar!
The titans remember me...
I am Man on Fire.
Today is training day!
I am the Batman,
I suddenly appear
in the Game of Thrones.
I remember the north.
I will redeem them like Shawshank.
I will avenge them with my Marvels;
When I enter the House of Black and White
It will crumbled like a House of Cards;
It will become the House of Rainbows.

Donning the Armour (after the Trump election)
By Adela Torchia

Easy now
to flinch and flail and fret
to lament the loss
of love and liberty.

Easy now to despair
or to decide to just not care.

Better still to don the armour
of grace and fortitude and valour.

No, we won't go!
Following like sheep
Or closing our eyes
and falling asleep.

Soldiers of valour
Warriors of victory
Refusing to step through
the trap door of history.

Down the dark path
of murderous misogyny
of rancid racism
and bedeviled bigotry.

Hell no, we won't go!!

Instead
donning the armour
of compassion and ardour
sharpening the sword
of love we move toward
the unceded territory
    of hope.

Rumi on Yates Street
By Torsten Schoeneberg

Behind a small red door on Yates Street

like those saloon doors in westerns

I saw a calendar "Rumi Illuminated 2017"

so I left my bike outside unlocked

and cast a glance.

I read Rumi saying (for July or so):

"*My soul is from elsewhere*

I'm sure of that

and I intend to end up there."

Another of his sayings was illustrated with

the Statue of Liberty shining a bright light and

you might not know I need a special visa to visit

the country of those westerns and that statue

exactly because I have visited the country of Rumi.

I pondered on buying the calendar as a present

but then saw it cost 20 dollars

said to myself "that's dinner" and left

got my bike

got distracted by beautiful legs crossing the street

passed a homeless man asking for change

didn't have change and

went to the bookshop and spent 36 dollars on

one book by Thomas Bernhard as a present

one book by Iain Banks for myself

rode away on Fort Street

thinking: what Rumi said will make me write

and having failed that homeless man will question my writing

and I'd like to talk about that if somebody asked

but no-one asks

they only ask what I think about Trump

but I think

shouldn't that be obvious?

At Mt. Baldy
By Angela Lee McIntyre

At Mt. Baldy, before the sesshin, someone mentioned that Leonard Cohen was going to attend.

I wondered how distracting that might be.

Would he be an entertaining seeker-of-attention, breaking into song as he served at silent meals, and, oh god! flirting?

We all wore our black robes, kept our eyes down and never spoke, so I needn't have worried.

I really had no idea if he was the student walking ahead of me, if those were his footsteps I followed in the snowy kinhin line.

I really had no idea where he sat in the zendo, or if he flirted.

I climbed onto my cushion, experienced what was there to experience, which was not Leonard Cohen's personality.

Later, in L.A., at Cimarron, he flipped some burgers at our after-retreat barbeque and offered me one.

Thanks, Leonard, I said.

Yogini

By Amy Nold

Aaaaaaooooooooommmmmmm
I'm a yogini, that's what I Am Aham
I practice Tantra and recite Mantra
And even learned how to do Tratak on Sri Yantra
I do Asanas combined with Bandhas
And I aSpire to the Yamas and Niyamas
Ahimsa, Asteya, Aparigraha, Brahmacharya,
Ta pas, Sau cha, San tosha, Svadyaya,
I practice Tapas, then take a nap as a Corpse in Shavasana
I got my Karma, M'aware Ma Dharma, I'm a Yogini, that's what Aham
I chant a Mantra and practice Tantra, do Pranayama to Anugama
I practice Neti but not Naula and even know some funky words in Pali
Muldhara, Svadishthana, Manipura, Anahata, Vischuddha, Ajna, Sahaswara Om
I want to reach Samadhi, I want to be Somebody like a fierce yogini lookin' good in a bikini
Then all the world will want to see me, then all the world will want to be me
Then I'll go hide in a cave, they'll all think I'm very brave
I'll sit on my tiger skin, and, no, you can't come in
I want to meditate, not medicate, my pain and fear away away ya way ya way ya way ya
I want to feel deep inner Shanthi shanthi shanthi Om
Aaaaaaooooooooommmmmmm

Stormborn

By Tariq Al Lamki

Daenerys Stormborn,
I was born of storms;
my eye starts forming-
whenever I feel cornered in.

Daenerys Stormborn,
I must warn I was born,
of remorseless wind.
I come in so many forms
like a formless Jin.

Who do they think they're cornering?

Morpheus?
Or-pheus?
Are we morphing?
Into a metamorphosis?
What sort of foreign metaphor is this?
I am morphing into a metamorphosis.

My throat is sore-
as the eye of the sorceress.
My eye is the open throat
of the lycanthrope.
My wings;
two burning chests.
I open wide.

I walk the earthen floor on all fours
like a foreign metaphor,
for I move like the flurry
of the Northern fist.
Can you feel the crack!
of my cordless whip?

Like a wild electric wire,
Of course it is;
sawing discord
to you coordinates.
How extraordinarily
inordinate;
I am morphing into a metamorphosis,
staring down the eye of the Occulus,
startling the mind of the Octopus.
I am alive in the eyes of the Optimus,
beating in the heart of the Populous.
I am back in the days of the Spartacus.
I have unlocked the heart of the Artemis-
lighting it up like an arsonist.

Daenerys,
blaze this Kriss
and make it kiss.
Engrave my wrists
with lists of names
in praise of bliss.
Engrave this glyph
till hills of haze,
cliffs of sulfur
mists and blaze,
are raised from my nasal rifts
in waves...
Deep intensity!
Each and every, entity-
entwist our flame
like fate and destiny.
Snakes will hiss,
"What kind of altered flame is this?"
This flame is Nameless
Stainlessness
The domain that it reign is
framelessness.
What can be gained in
painlessness?

Danerys Stormborn,
I forewarned I was born,
of remorseless wind.
I form and reform
like a formless Jin.
Oxy-gen!
Ingenious...
Akin to what a Jin
or a genie is!

Daenerys Stormborn,
I was born with thorns.

Daenerys Stormborn,
I was born with horns;
I am the Ox
in your oxygen.
Though I am your Anti
oxidant.
We come face to face
like Octahedra.
I am backed by the eight
of the Octagon.
I come across
the X-
 as the exorcist;
for I cut across
the S-
like the exodus
and ebb,
like Nibir
in the Nebulous.

Daenerys Stormborn,
I was born of men,
sworn and reborn
as your sword again.
I am the sun.
I set forth like the Red Northman
and cut to the source-
like a Norse swordsman,
when the force courses in,
I unhorse the Four Horsemen
and every man on a horse
with them-
they were warned
I was born of remorseless wind.
I come in so many forms
like a formless Jin.

Who did they think they were cornering?

Daenerys Stormborn,
I was born of storms;
my eye starts forming-
whenever you feel cornered in.

Daenerys Stormborn,
I was born of wind;
I start forming,
wherever,
you feel cornered in,
raising you high
like an ornament.

VII: SWEET LIGHT AND LOVE

Sweet Morning Tea
By Emily Krauss

Mornings are my favorite time of day
for I like to wake up to a brightly shining day
and pour myself a cup of hot steaming tea

I smell the tea
and let the aroma
surround me

Then slowly, slowly, slowly
I start to sip the tea
and savor its taste
until like magic
it has disappeared
and I am left with a feeling
of having enjoyed the tea
but also a feeling of
craving more tea

She Spreads Her Wings
By Terra Hawk

She spreads her wings

To greet the sun

Joyful with the morning come

Gilded golden

With first flight

Soaring to an awesome height

Comes to life

All things are one

Joyful, with the morning come

Light Rider
By Michelle Riddle

I am the line that divides the canvas.
I am the letter on the page.
I am the word, the song, the voice
That splits the day into field and sky
And pierces the night with stars.
A book filled with nothing,
A frame hung on the universe,
Boundless is my joy.

Untitled
By Serafina Christina

Your love leaves

A glitter trail

Hope; I follow

If I can turn

My love into

Silver too

You might just

Notice me.

his house for her (Alexander's Castle, Fort Worden, WA)
By Nancy Yakimoski

a wee Scottish castle
for his Scottish bride-to-be
that he'd fetch and bring after the war

a sword of a building
thrust deep into the hill
its three-storey hilt rising from the ground

a defiant edifice
that seemed to know
with every layer of brick and mortar
she would not be coming

a stubborn love, unyielding
to the inlet's winds and rain
and the passing of decades

>inside
>the walls and windows and stairs
>shift and rework the story
>without the happily ever after.

>outside,
>in front of its locked door
>I stand alone
>on the threshold

>alone
>at the threshold
>I whisper into weathered wood
>because I *need* to know:

>"Are you still in there, Love,
>without your beloved?"

Love Sparks
By Serafina Christina

Love shivers through my body

Leaving no trace of lies

I tell myself to stay small

It elevates me beyond reality

I find my smile wide

In the fresh empty space

Of a new mind presence

Of self knowledge and rightness

I am assured this is my way.

Speechless
By Sydney Pimiskern

My breasts heaved when you entered.
Lungs turned to gold.
Heart melted to my ribs.
My stomach angered to eat every inch of you.
And my lips longed to tell you how handsome you are.
My dress glided across the room,
Wanting to show herself off.
My feet fought to resist,
But it was helpless.
The rose on your suit sang softly to me.
Begging me to come near and sniff.
The closer I approached, the redder my cheeks blushed.
Your fingers danced across my face,
my chest,
my thigh.
Your teeth leaned toward me.
"Happy 30th anniversary my love"

October Reverie
By Peter Mancuso

Sitting outside, soaking in the sun,
Listening to music, having some fun.
Who knew an October Monday,
Could feel so like a Sunday?

New Act
By Amy Nold

Nothing is original,
At least that's what they say.
But tell me, doesn't each day bring
A new act upon the play?

Fools and Angels
By Amy Nold

Fools entrench in much and stench
while Angels dance by happenstance
till seen through by inversion
an intro and an extro version

Epiphany Kitchen
By Tariq Al Lamki

I'm trying to figure your secret recipe

like Martha Stewart,

but obsessively.

Must my heart keep breaking to *open*?

Sesame...

Tenth Planet Love
By Ibrahim Hazmi

توأمُ الرُّوحِ (Soul-Mate)
By Ibrahim Hazmi
Translation by Mohammed Ghazi Alghamdi

من أنتِ؟ في كلِّ الدروبِ أراكِ
وأراكِ في سهوي وفي إدراكي

وأراكِ في الأنهارِ، في خُضرِ الرُّبى
في البدرِ، في الآفاقِ، في الأفلاكِ

وأراكِ في كلِّ النِّسَاءِ، ولا أرى
فيهنَّ إلاّ ما ترى عيناكِ

يا توأمي، يا نصفَ روحي، يا أنا
يا خافقي الغضَّ الذي يَهْواكِ

يا صورتي في الماءِ، يا أسطورتي
يا قيمتي: أنا .. مَنْ أنـا؟ إلاّكِ

يا أروعَ استجداءِ روحي للمُنَى
يا أعذبَ استِلهَامِها نَجْواكِ

يا بردَ أيـامِ الصقيعِ ودفئَها
يا باقَةَ الأزهَارِ والأشـواكِ

يا جنَّةَ الأشواقِ .. يا نارَ الجَوَى
مَنْ لي بِمِثلِكِ، فِتنَتي وملاكِي

تستغربين .. أهيمُ فيكِ ولم تكُن
خطرتْ -على مرِّ الهوى- لُقْيَاكِ؟

عَيناكِ حدَّثتَـا : بـأنَّ لقـاءَنـا
سَبَقَتْهُ, في خُضرِ الجِنـانِ, رُؤاكِ

شَفَتاكِ أَوْمَأَتا : بِأَنَّكِ، توأمـي،
نادَيْتِني .. أنـا عاشِـقٌ لَبَّـاكِ

أنا لم أهِمْ بِسِواكِ عشقاً ساميـاً
أبداً .. ومَـا صَدَقَ الهَوَى لِسِوَاكِ

أنا ما عَرَفْتُ الحبَّ إلا حينمَـا
أبصرتُ رُوحي في وَمِيضِ سَنَاكِ

إنْ كنتِ في هذا الوُجودِ قصيدةً
أنا شاعرُ الحبِّ الذي غَنَّـاكِ

أوْ كنتِ في رَحْبِ الفَضاءِ مَجَرَّةً
أنا نَجْمُكِ الهادي الذي ضَوَّاكِ

أوْ كنتِ في قَعْرِ المُحيطِ مَحَـارَةً
أنا أعْيُنُ الغـوَّاصِ والسَّمّـاكِ

أوْكنتِ في الدِّينِ الحنيفِ شَعِيرَةً
أنـا أدمُـعُ العُبَّـادِ والنُّسَّـاكِ

للرُّوحِ توأمُها الوحيدُ ..
وللنَّوى أمدٌ ..
وإنِّي يافتـاةُ فَتَـاكِ

Who are you? I see you in every trail,
Unconsciously or not, I still see you

In the rivers, in the green hills,
In the full moon, in the horizon, and in the orbits

And I see you in all women but can't see,
In them except what you see,

Soul-mate, my half soul, myself,
my delicate loving heart,

my reflection in the water, my legend,
my merit: Who am I? But you!

my soul's delightful muse for wishes,
its sweet inspiration for your whispers

You're the cold freezing days and their warmth,
the flowers bouquet and their thorns

Yearnings' heaven, passion of fire,
Where to find like you, my angel

You wonder .. I'm obsessed with you
Yet never -before- have met you

Preceded, in the green land, by your visions
Your eyes said: that's our meeting

Your lips muttered: my soul-mate
 You called me . . And, I answered

Never been in a heavenly love but with you
Never...and how can love be true but to you

I never knew love until
I saw my soul flashing in your lightening

If you were a poem
Then I would be the poet of love singing you

If you were an orbit

Then I would be your guided star that twinkled you

If you were an oyster in the abyss of the ocean
Then I would be the eyes of the diver and the fisherman looking for you

Even if you were a religious ritual
Then I would be the tears of worshipers and monks, I love you!

There is a single mate for a soul. . .
And for the distance there is an end . . .
And I am your soul-mate!

(Saga of the Soul) أسطورةُ الرُّوحِ
By Ibrahim Hazmi
Translation by Mohammed Ghazi Alghamdi

أنا طيفُ ذكراها الذي تَتَجَاهَلُه
أنا حُلْمُها يَدْنو ولا تَتَنَاوَلُه

أنا بعضُ نجواها إذا هِيَ خافَتَتْ
أنا كلُّ شيءٍ ظاهرٍ تَتَدَاوَلُه

أنا صُبْحُها والعشقُ يزحفُ جَيشُهُ
أنا ليلُها تغفو لديَّ جَحَافِلُه

أنا صحوُ عينيها إذا رأتِ المُنَى
أنا غيمُها يروي المسَافَةَ وابِلُه

أنا عطرُ رَوضَتِها وزهرُ ربيعِها
أنا عذبُ لحنِ نشيدِها وبلابِلُه

أنا نفحُ كاذيها وطِيبُ خَطُورِه
أنا فلُّها تزهو عَلَيَّ جداثِلُه

أنا بحرُ كوكبِها وأُفْقُ فَضَائِها
أنا دينُها وفروضُهُ ونوافِلُه

أنا مَطْلَعٌ لقصيدةٍ في وصفها
أنا مُلهِمُ الشَّطرِ الأخيرِ وقائلُه

أنا رُغمَ كلِّ هروبِها مجنونُه
أنا عاقلُ الحبِّ الكبيرِ وجاهلُه

أنا لستُ بدعاً غيرَ أني عاشقٌ،
شَهِدَتْ عليه بما اعتراهُ أناملُه

أنَا حبُّها نُسكي وموكبُ حجِّها،
يطوي المناكبَ لا تَكَلُّ قوافلُه

واللهِ لو عَطِشَتْ فإنِّي ماؤها،
جداولُه يَكُونُ ما بأعذبِ تَجْري

I'm her ignored phantom of memory,
Her unclaimed approaching dream,

Some private talks she whispers,
Everything out there she lives with.

I'm the morning and the crawling army of passion
The night and its legion dozing for me

Her eyes seeing destiny
The clouds watering the distance heavily

The fragrance of her meadow and the spring flowers
The melody and the nightingales of her singing

The screw pine essence and the scent of her garlands
Her ringlet of jasmine growing on me

Her planet's orbit and the horizon of her space
Her religion, its obligations and voluntary deeds.

I am a prologue to her poem
A muse to its final verse and its writer

Despite her escapes, I'm her lunatic lover
The wise preacher of great love, and its naïve giver

Nothing new about me apart from being a lover, his fingers witnessed what happened to him

Her love is my monastic and the persistent convoys
of her pilgrimage procession folding the highlands

And God, if she thirsts, I'm her water,
Running fresh down stream.

(Siege ..) حصارٌ ..

By Ibrahim Hazmi
Translation by Talal Al Lamki, and Mohammed Alghamdi

قُبيلَ اقترابي، على غفلةٍ، من مَدَاك ..
أكانَ على الأرضِ أن تستديرَ إلى الخلفِ ..
أن تتباعد أسفارُنا ..
أو تمرَّ رياحي سراعاً ..
لتنأى مناي إذن عن مُنَاك؟

أكانَ على الأفق أن يتظاهرَ بالصّحوِ ..
كي لا يُؤرَّخَ بالغيثِ يومُ لِقاك؟

أكانَ على الوقتِ أن يأمُرَ العقربَيْنِ ..
بأنْ يقضيا ذلك اليومَ دونَ حِراك؟

ومنذُ البدايةِ ..
لمّا تَفتَّحَ زهري على قطرةٍ من نَداك ..
أكانَ عليَّ التنازلُ عن حاجتي للحياةِ ..
وما عدتُ أحيا سوى كي أراك؟
أكانَ عليَّ الهلاك ؟..!

مساءَ التقينا،
وفاحَ، بأعذبِ ما لم يُخيَّل إليَّ، شذاك
أكانَ عليَّ اعتزالي ..
وكانَ على نورِ عينيكِ ألا يجوسَ خِلالي ..
وكانَ على كلِّ شيءٍ حَوالَيَّ،
أن يتجاهلَ ومضَ سناك؟

أكانَ عليَّ الجلوسُ بعيداً ..
ولا فرق – حيثُ تكونين – بين هنا أو هناك؟

أكانَ عليَّ التشاغُلُ عنكِ ..
وأنتِ تطوفين حول حدائق عينيّ مثل الملاك ؟

أكانَ على أذنيّ التعذّر منكِ ..
وأنتِ تقولين ما لا توَدّين أنك قلتِ،
لئلا أعيشَ بذكرى صداك ؟

أكانَ على الشاي أن يتخثّرَ قبل بلوغِ فمي،
حينما قدّمتهُ يداك؟

وحين اعترفتُ بأنكِ ملهمةُ الشعرِ،
من عهدِ آدمَ حتى نشبتُ بذاتِ الشِّراك
أكانَ على الشعر أن يتمرّدَ ..
ألاّ يطبعَ تولّعَ حرفي بذكركِ ..
ألاّ يؤمَّ حِمَاك؟

أكانَ على الحاء والباء،
أن يهجرا أحرفَ الأبجديةِ ..
أن يذهبا،
حيثُ لا يتمنطقُ حلقي ولا تلتقي شفتاك؟

وحين تذرَّعتِ بالذكرياتِ ..
ومستقبلُ الروح بعضُ رضاكِ ..
أكانَ عليَّ تفاديَ سهام الهوى،
والنُّجومُ وكلُّ الوجوه تشيرُ إليَّ بأنّي فَتَاكِ؟
أكانَ عليَّ إدانةُ روحي التي صَدَّقَتْ ..
أن ثمةُ توأمَ روح لها فيكِ لا في سواكِ ؟
أكانَ عليَّ بأن أتجاوَزَ كلَّ القواميسِ،
أوْ أتَنَكَّبَ كلَّ النواميس ..
حتى أكونَ -وأنّى أكونُ- أخاكِ ؟

أكانَ عليَّ بأن أقضيَ العمرَ،
في ردهاتِ القصورِ ..
أُفَتِّشُ في كلّ أنثى هنالك عنكِ،
وعمّا أسميهِ — عَجزاً — هواكِ؟

وبعدُ .. وعشقي الجنونيُّ أبعدُ من منتهاكِ ..
أَكَانَ عَليَّ حصَارُكِ،
حتى تُكذّبَ عَيناكِ لونَ الحقيقةِ ..
حَتَّى تُشَكِّكَ في دَرْبِ حُبّي خُطَاكِ؟

Right before approaching your space ..
Must earth reverse its rotation,
And our travels diverge,
Or must my wind blow,
Separating my hopes from yours?

Must the horizon fake clarity,
Lest it chronicles us on a rainy day?

Must the clock demand its hands,
To stay still on that day?

And since the beginning,
When my flowers blossomed by your dew ..
Must I give up life,
Since I'm only alive to see you?
Or must I perish?

The night we met,
When your aroma, sweeter than my wildest imagination
Should I've abandoned myself?
Shouldn't your eyes have penetrated me?
Or should everything around me have ignored you?

Should I've sat faraway?
Where you are, it doesn't matter where I set!

Should I have busied myself,
When you were wandering, like an angel,
Around my eyes?

Should I've shut my ears,
When you were speaking?
Then lamenting to me,
Lest I live the memory of your echo?

When you poured me tea,
Should it have clotted?

And when I confessed:
Since the time of Adam, "you're the poetic muse"
Must poetry have rebelled,
And disobeyed the passion of my letters towards you,
Or refused to enter your heaven?

Must the L's and V's (LoVe)
Leave the Alphabet,
And reside in my parallelized tongue,
Or perhaps, freeze at your lips?

When my past was your excuse,
And my future depends on your approval,
Must've I dodged the darts of love,
Whilst the stars and all faces point to me, your hero?
Must've I convicted my soul,
That found a soulmate in no one but you?
Must've I ignored all dictionaries,
Or violated the laws of nature,
Becoming your brother,

Must've I spent life wandering the halls of castles,
Searching, in every woman, for you and what I call "love"?

Then, when my insane wild love transcends your limits,
Must've I sieged you,
Till your eyes are blinded to see the color of truth,
Or till your steps doubt the pathway to my love?

(Disappointments of "Whys") خيبةُ الأسئلةِ

By Ibrahim Hazmi
Translation by Talal Al Lamki, Mohammed Alghamdi,
and Ibrahim Hazmi

لماذا مررتُ بتلكَ الخيامِ البعيدة؟
لماذا تصديتُ وحدي لتلكَ الرياحِ العنيدة؟

لماذا خرجتُ من القبرِ ..
والمتصرِّفُ في الناسِ ..
مازالَ يمنحُهم صَكَّ غُفرانه ..
أو يصبُّ عليهم وعيدَه؟

لماذا ابتعدتُ،
إلى حدِّ أدركتُ ..
أن المسافة بين الحقيقةِ والشّرقِ،
بضعُ قرونٍ عتيدة؟

وأنَّ المسافاتِ بين الشّعوبِ ..
كمثل المسافات بين الكواكبِ ..
لاتتلاشى ولو قُرِّبَتْ في سطورِ جريدة؟

لماذا اقتربتُ إلى منتهى سكرةِ العشقِ ..
حتّى رأيتُكِ أنتِ الوحيدة ..

لماذا كتبتُكِ؟
ليتَكِ ما كُنتِ أنتِ القصيدة ..

لماذا ادّرعتُ هواكِ وبيني ..

وبينَ اجتراحِ الصِّبا أن أُريدَه؟

لماذا اعترفتُ بكلِّ الحقيقةِ ..
والليلُ يمنحُ سرِّي بريده؟

لماذا وُلدتُ بذاتِ المسَاءِ الذي ..
شيّعَ الصِّدقُ فيه الحكايا الوليدَة ..

لماذا نشأتُ بذاتِ المكانِ الذي ..
استنكرَ الوأدُ فيهِ ازدحامَ النُّفوسَ الوئيدة ..

لماذا ؟
إلهي اعفُ عني ..
فقلبي يحبُّكَ -رغم الخطايا العديدة-
ولكنْ أحلامَ روحي نأت بي ..
إلى حيثُ يجتازُ عقلي حدوده .

Why did I pass by those distant tents?
Why did I, alone, face those wild winds?

Why did I crawl out of my grave,
When the joker still grants pardons,
Or pours vengeance?

Why have I gone too far,
Realizing how the East is distanced,
From the truth?

And the gap between nations,
Like the distance between planets,
Can't vanish even if printed together in a paper?

Why have I been too close,
Romantically intoxicated,
Till I saw no one but you?

Why have I composed you?
I wish you weren't the poem!

I could've enjoyed guilt,
Have I not shielded myself with love?

Darkness could've kept my secrets away,
Have I not confessed the whole truth?

Why was I born the same night,
When truth carried innocent tales to graves?

Why was I raised where infanticide, the crime itself,
Was choked by the infinite suicidal souls?

Why?
God, forgive me,
Despite my transgressions, I still love You,
It's my irrational soul dreaming,
Forcing my mind beyond its edges.

(As you wish) قولي كما شئتِ

By Ibrahim Hazmi
Translation by Talal Al Lamki, Mohammed Alghamdi,
and Ibrahim Hazmi

قولي كما شئتِ ما عادت بأيدينا
ولم تَعُدْ قَسوةُ الأيّامِ تُصْبِينَا

ولم يَعُدْ في دماءِ الحبِّ أيُّ قذاً
ولم تَعُدْ وَشْوَشَاتُ اليأسِ تُؤذِينَا

لا وقتَ إلاَّ لروحي فيكِ تعرفُني
وللمجانينِ يلقَوْنَ المجانينَا

يا أعذبَ الماءِ إلا حينَ أشربُه
لم الطُّعُونُ طعونُ الدَّهرِ تَكفِينَا

لم المراحلُ كَمْ في العُمْرِ مرحلةٌ
لم المسافاتُ شِبْرُ الحبِّ يُؤوِينَا

إنَّا وروحُ الهَوَى تَروي جوانِحَنَا

وتَسكُبُ الشَّوقَ طُهراً في مآقِينَا

لا نَستقيلُ ولانَلوي أَعِنَّتَنَا
ولا نُبَدِّلُ غُصنَ البَانِ سِكِّينَا

كنّا الخليَّينِ نَسقي الخِلَّ من دمنا
فهل نَضِنُّ وأصْبَحْنَا المحبِّينَا

نحنُ الهُدى أورقتْ فينا خمائلُه
فلم يرَ الحبُّ خيراً من تدانينَا

أنسامُ مكَّةَ ما زالتْ تداعبُنا
ونورُ طيبةَ لم يخفُتْ بوادينَا

والمُتَّهمونَ بصُبْحِ العِشْقِ إخوتُنا
والمُنْجِدُونَ بِلَيلِ الوَجدِ أهلونَا

والملهماتُ رقيقَ الشِّعرِ نسوتُنا
هل تطربُ الأرضُ إلا حينَ يمشينَا

يا أصدقَ الحبِّ حظُّ الحبِّ أفئدةٌ
خضراءُ أصحابُها للحبِّ راعونَا

الحبُّ محرابُ أرواحٍ بها شغفٌ
لتجعلَ الصِّدقَ في أعماقنا دينَا

ألم يزلْ بعدُ للشكِّ المريبِ دجىً
يبدي ملائكةَ الدنيا شياطينَا

ألم ترَي قبلُ أنَّ الشمسَ ما غربت
إلا لتخلُدَ في النجوى ليالينَا

وما أطلَّ سناها بعدَ غيبتِهِ
إلا لتشرقَ حبًّا طاهراً فينَا

يا توأمَ الرُّوحِ ما عادَ الهوى ترفاً
سَلي عن الدمعِ أحداقَ المصلِّينَا

ما عادِ للصَّمتِ في الآذان مُتَّسَعٌ
قولي كما شئتِ ما عادت بأيدينَا

Say as you wish, it's out of our hands,
And the rough days are over.

This love is Platonic,
Where despair has no place.

Time is dying,
Waiting for mad souls to unite,
And in you, still my half soul resides.

You're the sweetest water,
Yet I can't drink.
Isn't that enough?

You are closer to Love!
Why climb all these steps?

I'm from where love nourishes souls,
filling eyes with joyful tears.

My people are not quitters,
Nor cowards!

We would share blood to rescue friends,
Let alone when they're soulmates.

We're "Love's Chosen People."

Still, the breeze from Mecca blesses us,
And the light from Taiba shines our valley,

We're from Tehama, the spring of love.
Where rhythms are born as women gait

How lucky is "Love"
When it's Platonic ?

Love is the *Mihrab* of passionate souls,
Preaching honesty.

Can't you see the difference,
Between Angles and Devils?

Didn't you see that the sun hides everyday,
Only to paint our nights with spiritual intimacy?
Then shines to flourish our souls with love.

My soulmate,
Love isn't a luxury!
Confirmed by tears of worshipers.

There is no place for silence!
Say as you wish, it's out of our hands.

(Standing At My Grave) قبري على وقفةٌ

By Ibrahim Hazmi
Translation by Mohammed Ghazi Alghamdi

ما زلتُ أبحثُ عن ظلّي الذي غابا
وأرسلُ الطّيرَ في ذكرايَ أسراباً

حتى رحلتُ وكانَ العمرُ مغترباً
وكنتُ في عرصَاتِ العشقِ أوّاباً

يا رُبَّ طارقةٍ بابي وقد نَسِيَتْ
أني قضيتُ شبابي أطرقُ البابا

ورُبَّ مقبلةٍ نحوي وقد يَئِسَتْ
منها الدُّروبُ وخطوي نحوها خابا

ورُبَّ شارقةٍ والشّمسُ قد غربت
ونورُ عينيَّ عن عينيَّ قد غابا

ورُبَّ مبحرةٍ والعمرُ قد سكنتْ
رياحُهُ وهديرُ العشقِ قد ذابا

حلمُ الطفولةِ أجَّلتيه وا أسفا
وكنتُ أقربَ من حُلْمَينِ أو قابا

ألم يكنْ في يديكِ الأمرُ سيِّدتي
أم غرَّكِ الدمعُ مني فاض تسكابا

وسرَّ عينيكِ ذُلِّي في مطاردتي
أطيافَ روحِكِ واستعذبْتِ لي الصابا

وملَّ سمعُكِ من صوتي الذي طربتْ
له الجميلاتُ واستهدى به "البابا"

ألم تريْ أنَّها الأيَّامُ شاهدة
أنتِ التي للهوى حطَّمْتِ أعتابا

وأنتِ أنتِ التي كذَّبتِ أشرعتي
وأنتِ من أنكصَ المجنونَ أعقابا

وأنتِ أنتِ التي قصَّصتِ أجنحتي
وأنتِ من صيَّرَ الأهلينَ أغرابا

إني قضيتُ حياتي في مجاهدةٍ
ولم أكن لحظةً في العشقِ مرتابا

سكنتُ في السُحبِ حتى لا تُجَرِّحَني
سهامُ صدِّكِ، إنِّي عشتُ هيَّابا

أخشى عليكِ -قضيتُ العمرَ- من قَوَدي
ومن أسى حسرةٍ تمتدُّ أحقابا

ودَّعتُ دنياكِ يا فردوسَ آخرتي
طابَ الهوى ومقامُ الصبِّ ما طابا

هل ترتجينَ لضيفِ القبرِ عودتهُ
واللهِ ماكانَ إلاَّ الموتُ غلَّابا

لقد رضيتُ هوانَ العشقِ ما بقيتْ
روحي وكنتُ لدارِ السُّهدِ بواباً

وقد تأخرتِ يا من كانَ كلُّ دمي
يفدي ثراكِ وعنكِ الخلدُ قد نابا

فادعي لعلّ لقاءَ الخلدِ يجمعُنا
واستغفري العشقَ،
طوبى للذي تابا

Still looking for my absent shadow
Sending flocks of birds in my memorial

Until I left, life was an exile
And repentant I was from the vacuum of love

She comes knocking my door, perhaps, forgetting
I've spent my youth knocking hers

She comes toward me, perhaps, yet my trails
Gave up and my steps toward her failed

Like her sun rising when mine was set
And the light of my eyes was out

She is sailing, perhaps, when the wind
of life was silent and the fire of love has become ashes

The childhood dream, alas, you've suspended
When I was closer to both dreams, or almost there

My lady, wasn't in your hand
Or did you take my pouring tears for granted

Or were you delighted to watch my meekness,
 Following your mirage,
And you were entertained by it

Or were you bored to hear my melodic voice
That seduced beautiful girls and guided "the Pope"

Don't you see that days witnessed
how you've demolished beginnings of love

And you, it's you who denied my beliefs,
Worsening my lunacy

And you, it's you who clipped my wings
estranging relatives

I've spent life in struggle
Never for a moment was I skeptic of love

Taking shelter in the clouds away from your sharp
arrows, I lived frightfully

I fear for you -as long as I lived- from guilt,
From a long lasting anguish

I abandoned your world, my hereafter paradise,
Love was pleased, not the lover

Do you wish for the grave's resident return
God, it was the dominance of death

If my soul stayed, I would accept the humiliating love,
I would be a guard for the home of insomnia

You were late, replaced by eternity,
When I would sacrifice all of my blood to water your earth

Pray that our meeting in immortality unites us
And ask redemption from love,
Blessed is the repented one!

بُرُودٌ .. (Iceberg)
By Ibrahim Hazmi
Translation by Mohammed Ghazi Alghamdi

لم يعد يقلقُني الردُّ..
ولا يوجعني البعدُ..
ولا يقتلني الإجحافُ أوالصدُّ..

حياتي ..
لم يَعُد يحكمُها الجزرُ أوالمدُّ..

فقد أصبحتُ حرًّا..

وعلى رغمِ افتقارِ الرُّوحِ..
للرُّوح التي تعرفُها..
ذاتي التي تسكنُها..

ما عدتُ أبكي كلما حدقتُ في مغربِ شمسٍ..
لم توّدعني مساءاً أو تقبّلني صباحاً

كلُّ ما أفعلُه
أكتُبُهَا. .
أكتُبُني...

أتخفّى
حينما قطرُ الندى – في مُقلتي - يَغلِبني...

وأواري أحرفي قبراً ..
من الأسلاكِ والموجاتِ لا آمنُه غدراً ومكراً

وعلى كلٍّ.....
فإني لم أكن أو دعته للحب سرّا

أخطر الأسرار أني...
لستُ أنوي العيشَ مثل الناسِ..
أو مثل النصوصْ
حمّالَ وجوهٍ

-أو كما في معجمي- مثلَ اللصوصْ!

فلقدْ اصبحتُ حُرًّا

Awaiting response doesn't distress me anymore,
Nor does remoteness hurt me,
Or injustice or avoidance kill me.

My life .
Isn't anymore controlled by ebb and flow,

I became free

Despite the longing of my soul
to the soul it knows
to myself that dwells in it

I don't cry anymore gazing at the sun,
It doesn't wish me good night nor good morning.

All what I do,
I compose her..
I compose me..

I hide sometimes,
When drops of rain-in my eyes-comes pouring
I hide my letters in a tomb
of untrusted wicked wires and currents …

Anyhow ..
I haven't trusted it with love

The most dangerous secret, I intend
Not to live like people,
Or verses,
All alike disguised wearing multiple faces
-According to my dictionary- like thieves

As I'm free.

قولي كما شئت (Mutiny)

By Ibrahim Hazmi

Translation by Mohammed Alghamdi, Tala Al Lamki, and Ibrahim Hazmi

إذا جئتَ تُسنِدُ ظهركَ:
تُغمِضُ عينيكَ,
تأخذُ أعمقَ أنفاسِ عمركَ,
تُرخي جميعَ مفاصلِ قلَبِك,
توحي لكل خلاياكَ ..
أن تتهيّأ للعوم
في لا نهايةِ غَورِ الفضاء

هل تتوقّعُ أنّك تُسنِده للهواء؟

هل اتسعَ البُعْدُ بين الدقائق عُمرا
وهل غِبتَ عن وعي حُبّكَ شزراً
وهل غادرَ العابرونَ أماكنَهُم
قبل ألا يقولَ سليمانُ للجُند أمراً
ليستحضروا عرشَ بلقيسَ
في طَرفةٍ من دهاء؟

ألا تعلمينَ؟
بأنّكِ أولُ قارعةٍ ..
تتجرأ أن تطرقَ البابَ ..
تعصي قوانينَ عشقِ التوائمْ ..

والله ما كانَ يوصِدهُ ..
غيرُ خوفي عليكُنّ ..
أن تتشظّيْنَ مِمّا بداخله من مآتم ..

وها أنتِ أدركتِ أنَّ المغارمَ
تَغلِبُ في مثل حبّي المغانم

وها أنا أُقتَلُ قتلاً جديداً
يَزيدُ بجدرانِ قلبي المعالم

وها نحنُ ندخلُ فصلاً غريباً
ونجهلُ كيف تكون الخواتِم

أحقًّا ألومُكِ أنتِ التي لا
تخافين في الحُبّ لومةَ لائم

Before leaning back,
I close my eyes,
Taking the deepest breaths of my life,
Relaxing all the muscles of my heart,
Preparing every cell of mine,
To dive into the infinite space,

Do I imagine leaning back against a vacuum?

Has the span between minutes expanded?
Have I, for a moment, lost consciousness of my love?
Have passengers changed their seats,
Before Solomon commands his soldiers,
To retrieve Bathsheba's throne,
In a magical blink?

Don't you know?
That you're the first visitant,
Daring to knock on my door,
Rebellious against the laws of my love,

I've just locked my heart out of fear for you,
Its tragedies would shatter you

And now you realize,
How, in love, pain defeats gain!
And how I'm slain again and again,

And now without a compass,
We've taken a new road,

Should I blame you,
When you're fearless of love?

(The difference between you) ما الفرقُ بينكما ؟!‏ ..

By Ibrahim Hazmi
Translation by Ibrahim Hazmi, and Mohammed Alghamdi

ألمَ تتورَّطا فيما تُسمِّيه القِمَار؟
هو قال لي ما قلتَ، بلْ
وصلتْ إلى بابي أناملُه
وكانَ يقولُ لي وحدي،
الحكاياتِ الكِثار ..

أنتَ اختصرتَ العشقَ " تَمثيليَّةً " ..
تلهو بأفئدةِ النساء المنهكاتِ،
لدى طوابير القطار ..

ونَفَذْتَ لي منها،
وخدَّرتَ الأنوثةَ فيَّ
أيقظْتَ احتياجي في ليالي وحدتي،
لونَ النَّهار ..

ووعدتني بالخلدِ في عينيكَ
حتى لم أعُدْ من أي فاتنةٍ أغار ..

ونسيتُ أنَّك حينما أعطيتني يمناكَ
قُلتَ بأنَّ في يسراكَ قائمةَ انتظار ..

هو خانَ عينَ الفجر،
مختبأً بظلِّ الليلِ،
متّكئاً على ما كانَ بينكُما من القصص القصار ..

أنا لم أقُلْ للشمسِ: لا تثقي بآفاقِ التوهُّج
ثُمَّ أنكِرْ ظلَّ أوزاري على جسدي المُثَار ..

أنا لم أنادِ الليلَ ..
أتلُ الحزنَ في عينيكِ أحلاماً
لأحظى بانتظارِك – عندَ بابي – فتحَ نافذةِ الحِوار ..

نحن ارتضينا،
أن نعيشَ ببلدةِ الأشباحِ

نسبُرَ في شتاءِ الوهمِ أشباه البحار ..

ألا نعرِّضَ وردَنا للشَّمسِ
نتلوَ عند ناصيةِ المشاعرِ بعضَ أورادِ الوَقار ..

كانت بأيدينا الحياةُ – ولم تزلْ –
تدعو إلى طُهرِ الطُفولة من يُسمَّوْنَ "الكبارْ" ..

الفرقُ بينكما: توقفتِ المياهُ بنهرِها في أوَّلِ المشوارِ ..
أنكرتِ الحصار ..

أنتِ ارتآكِ غيابُها نَهراً
وقلبَكِ قارباً ..
يضعُ الأماني الخضرَ في شَبَكِ القرار ..

هي لم ترحّبْ بالرِّياح
لأنَّها تخشى اندلاعَ الحُبِّ من شَررِ الغُبار ..

هي -رغمَ تشريدي- أبتْ
أن تستجيرَ من اغترابِ العُمرِ بالوطنِ المُعار ..

هي -رغمَ تجريحي- استحقَّ سِنانُها الممتدُّ
من صدري إلى قبري مواجهةَ افتِخار ..

والفرقُ عندي أنَّني: ما عاد يزعجُني إذا قالتْ:
بأنَّ هواي ليس سوى مُحاولةِ انتحار ..

Didn't you gamble with your lives?
Like you , he narrated the same tales ,
Yet, his fingers painted my nails,
And while alone with him, I heard more and more.

Like a theatrical play—you dramatized love:
Abusing the hearts of tired women,
Who queue inline for a life train!

By that dramatic scene, you impressed me
Numbing my femininity ,
Awakening—during nights of loneliness— my need for a colorful day . . .

Promising me eternity inside your eyes,
Till I'm never jealous of any beautiful woman,

How did I forget when I shook your hand
Your confession of a waiting list in the other one?

Allow me to clarify:

Concealed by the shadow of darkness,
Fleeing the dawn,
Hiding between short tales,
he betrayed you.

Unlike him, I didn't persuade the sun
to trust the horizon,
I didn't deny the shadow of my sins,
Reflected on my shape.

I didn't call the nightfall,
To recite verses of sorrow,
To conjure your dreams.
I didn't wait for you
at my door.

You and I chose to live in a ghost town,
Like sailing, during winter, in a stormy ocean.
We chose to cover our flowers from sunshine,
muting our souls from singing hymns. . .

Wasn't life, and still is, in our hands,
Calling, the like of us, for innocence.

Yet, the difference between you and her:
She refused my siege at the earliest glimpse,
And the flow of her river has stopped ever since,

In her absence, emerged your flowing river,
Like an old boat, your heart revived hopes,
Yet demanded vows.

Unlike you, she resisted my winds,
Afraid that love sparks fire,

She chose exile
Over me, her imaginable home.

Yet, I relish her noble battle:
Cutting through me with a sharp spear
Dragging me closer to my grave.

And the difference that matters now:
I'm not bothered any more,
When she says: "you love is suicidal!"

خلودٌ .. (Eternity)

By Ibrahim Hazmi
Translation by Mohammed Ghazi Alghamdi

كنتِ وحدَكِ ..

ما كانَ يخطُرُ في الرُّوحِ إلاّكِ ..
ما كانَ يحلمُ بالحبِّ حتاكِ ..

أوجبتكِ المقاديرُ حلماً ..
يبلِّغُني ..
عالمَ الخُلدِ – سَكْرَةَ لقياكِ-

يلقِّنُني في المساءاتِ ..
أعذبَ نجواكِ ..

يباركُني ..
حينَ أعلنُ في مسمعِ الكونِ:
"أهوااااكِ"

خرافيَةَ الصّمتِ..
أسطورةَ الصَّدِّ..
معجزةَ الوصْل..
ماذا تبقى بتوراةِ نفيكِ – أشهاكِ –

اليومَ تغزو أناجيلَ حبِّكِ..
بعضُ المزاميرِ..
تبحثُ عن ظلّ أورادِها..
في ثناياكِ..

ما زِلتِ وحدَك..

لا زلتُ أحفظُ آياتِ عشقِكِ..
أشدو تراتيلَها في صلاتي..
بمحرابِ ذِكراكِ ..

You were the only one!

Nothing entertained my soul but you.
Me in love was a dream for many, even you

Yet,
Destiny forced you to be a dream;
 Delivers me,
 To the world of eternity -the intoxication of meeting you-

Soothes me at nights,
With the best of your sweet talks,

Blesses me,
When I announce to the entire world:
"I LOVE YOU"

A myth of silence
A tail of avoidance
An impossible soul-mate
What else is there in your Biblical rejections?

Today, my Biblical love is invaded
By some flutes
Looking for the shadows of their notes
In your absence.

Still, you're the only one!

I keep memorizing my Quranic love verses about you,

Reciting them in my prayers
At the *mihrab* of your memorial

VIII: AT LAST, WORDS

Spade

By Katherine Hewko

Spade
Dig down
Unearth roots, bones,
Secrets: turn them out
Into the light of judgement
Like pale potatoes clotted with earth
Shake free the shameful clinging insects and
The exhaustion of the filthy unborn harvest, now
Ripped forth like MacDuff to destroy a hollow tyrant

Petals

By Farah Percival

Her petals

So gentle

Her voice

So soft

Her words

Poetic

More beautiful than any rose

Silence
By Rosalind Taylor

Silence

and

Words

a vast chandelier

as wide as the sky,

made of light

and insect wings

too weightless to catch

or name,

iridescent and shining out

in all directions,

and

Silence

Heart

Here

every mantra in every language,

the sub-sonic boom

of stones and stars

Two with the Word "Carve"
By A.S. Chan

I: Active Retirement

Leant lame on a cane,
Proud legs begged a third,
Bucked from wild withers
Of summits deferred;

Now crown wreathed with rime,
I scale the occurred,
So stalk storm-carved verse,
Belayed on sheer word.

II: Instruction

Each day I'm lesser here
As I grow large elsewhere,
So I may not miss me
When I come not to be.

None then need carve a stone;
Let me, with other bone,
All namelessly be blent
The same as where I went.

Reverse Blade
By Tariq Al Lamki

Blaze liquid,

with licked and glazed

encrypted phrase

cryptic, unscripted.

Depicted as blade evicted this.

Predict-

this evicted blade as depicted:

Unscripted, cryptic

phrase encrypted.

Glazed and licked with

liquid-blaze.

Ode to Frost
By Michelle Riddle

Through a glass

Laced white with mist

I saw a land that slept

Under a spell

That frost had kissed

And winter neatly kept.

Not a leaf

Lay out of place,

Nor boulder marred the view,

Of this scape

Where tree lines traced

Paths paved by tired few.

forefinger and thumb
By Rosalind Taylor

writing from the palm of my hand,

the distance between my thumb and

forefinger, the distance between you

and me, the length, sense, entrance,

like a kite, the wind in my hair,

in the coral lungs expanding,

a whisper from you to change the

shape of the air around me, breath

that sweeps a butterfly over the

sweet smelling thyme, along the path

like a snake or a vein, blue with

intent, the course through a life

the gray hair, the long teeth,

pasture of horses, manes of fire

and wheat, grains of sand

by the waves, repeating, complete,

indistinguishable from the distance

between my forefinger and thumb.

Swoon
Angela Lee McIntyre

Inside the landscape
everything went still
fell away as I sat
on the edge of M's bed
reading sexy text messages
from you, out loud to her —
I might explode.

Now, on the ferry, a stranger, a man
with a suitcase, sits
one over, across from me
Is it obvious
that I'm contorted with yearning
as I read your text messages?
Do they notice how my fingers and toes
yearn for completion —
meaning you to hang onto?

In my seat I swoon, oh!
heat and electricity
run the length of me
flow from the bottom,
from the bottom
to the top, to the top

of all that is

or ever could be

that which permeates being

that which lives under this sea

beneath me now as I cross it —

all that I have ever known

with tongue, eye, skin, ear,

lung, is with me now

collapsed into one,

none, and all

Later I'm stunned by a vision of him:

a sad, 12-year-old boy, sunburned and complete

grows up alone, with mother and brother

knowing, but beyond knowing

I don't know, I don't know, I don't know,

pierces the sunburned dream

complete and beyond all knowing.

The man I can handle, it's the boy I worry about.

Is fuck me the call of the doomed,

the finished, the pessimistic

or the gloriously prepared?

Fuck me, those famous last words,

smell of salty cum, saliva, oil paint

and sweat, can occur as a sheer

white curtain taking on the wind

and losing.

Fuck me,
I'm screwed, I'm headed down a track
with no brakes.

Fuck me, I've been overtaken
by the sound of my own breathing.

Fuck me,
I can't stop saying 'I love you.'

Fuck me,
infinity is within it.

Fuck me,
you are no more lost than I am.

Fuck me,
you are a gift I've given myself ;
I didn't know I was that smart.

Fuck me, eternal embrace.

Fuck me, light.

Fuck me, dark.

Solitary Traveller
By Michelle Riddle

Solitary traveller

Watching people pass by

So many unknown passengers

Intersecting now to fly

To untold destinations

Exotic and mundane

With hurried gesticulations

They rush to board their plane

Yet through the clash and clatter

Like a deep and peaceful rill

Sits the solitary traveller

Watching people still

blessing name
By Rosalind Taylor

I have a name for you
though it has no sound
I have a name for you
brushed onto fine paper
character for you
I can't quite read
but know so well

You lie in the ink
stained under my nails
ink from a letter
I once wrote to you
writing your name
the secret name
that you can't hear

I am conjuring you
in a vanishing book
on a thin white page
I am conjuring you
with quick black marks
your structure intact
your memory here

I have tried to tell you
how the brush strokes
lie on the page of your name
still you come where the line
sinks echoing/ lost
just below my tongue
where it has no sound

INDEX OF AUTHORS

Al Lamki, Tariq 63, 70, 82, 116

Chan, A.S. 115

Christina, Serafina 29, 77, 79

Hawk, Terra 2, 9, 76

Hazmi, Ibrahim 83, 86, 88, 92, 94, 97, 101, 103, 105, 108

Hewko, Katherine 14, 62, 12

Johnston, Tina 48

Krauss, Emily 5, 8, 75

Levven, Delaney 24, 54

Macmillan, Daymon 28

Mancuso, Peter 17, 33, 34, 35, 36, 37, 38, 81

McIntyre, Angela Lee 3, 41, 60, 68, 119

Nold, Amy 51, 53, 56, 69, 81

Percival, Farah 6, 14, 16, 34, 50, 55, 113

Pimiskern, Sydney 7, 13, 30, 52, 80

Riddle, Michelle 10, 11, 15, 36, 43, 45, 46, 77, 117, 122

Shoeneberg, Torsten 20, 22, 66

Taylor, Rosalind 7, 12, 18, 33, 35, 40, 44, 114, 118, 123

Torchia, Adela 64

Yakimoski, Nancy 4, 23, 37, 78

www.ingramcontent.com/pod-product-compliance
Lightning Source LLC
Chambersburg PA
CBHW072203100526
44589CB00015B/2344